S0-AFV-387

Houghton Mifflin Harcourt

Getting Ready for the
Smarter Balanced
Assessment

INCLUDES

- Common Core Standards Practice in SBAC format
- Beginning-, Middle-, and End-of-Year Benchmark Tests with Performance Tasks
- Year-End Performance Assessment Task

Contents

Common Core Assessment Formats

Common Core Assessment consortia have developed assessments that contain item types beyond the traditional multiple-choice format. This allows for a more robust assessment of students' understanding of concepts. Common Core assessments will be administered via computers; and *Getting Ready for the Smarter Balanced Assessment* presents items in formats similar to what you will see on the tests. The following information is provided to help familiarize you with these different types of items. Each item type is identified on pages (vii–viii). The examples will introduce you to the item types. The following explanations are provided to guide you in answering the questions. These pages describe the most common item types. You may find other types on some tests.

Example 1 Tell if a number rounds to a given number.

Yes or No

For this type of item, you respond to a single question with several examples. There are directions similar to, "For numbers 1a–1d, choose Yes or No to tell whether …" Be sure to answer the question for each part given below the directions. Fill in the bubble next to "Yes" or "No" to tell whether the example fits the description in the question. You must fill in a bubble for each part.

Example 2 Identify examples of a property.

More Than One Correct Choice

This type of item looks like a traditional multiple-choice item, but it asks you to mark all that apply. To mark all that apply, look for more than one correct choice. Carefully look at each choice and mark it if it is a correct answer.

Example 3 Circle the word that completes the sentence.

Choose From a List

Sometimes when you take a test on a computer, you will have to select a word, number, or symbol from a drop-down list. The *Getting Ready for the Smarter Balanced Assessment* tests show a list and ask you to choose the correct answer. Make your choice by circling the correct answer. There will only be one choice that is correct.

Example 4 Sort numbers by even or odd.

Sorting

You may be asked to sort something into categories. These items will present numbers, words, or equations on rectangular "tiles." The directions will ask you to write each of the items in the box that describes it. When the sorting involves more complex equations or drawings, each tile will have a letter next to it. You will be asked to write the letter for the tile in the box. Sometimes you may write the same number or word in more than one box. For example, if you need to sort quadrilaterals by category, a square could be in a box labeled rectangle and another box labeled rhombus.

Example 5 Order numbers from least to greatest.

Use Given Numbers in the Answer

You may also see numbers and symbols on tiles when you are asked to write an equation or answer a question using only numbers. You should use the given numbers to write the answer to the problem. Sometimes there will be extra numbers. You may also need to use each number more than once.

Example 6 Match related facts.

Matching

Some items will ask you to match equivalent values or other related items. The directions will specify what you should match. There will be dots to guide you in drawing lines. The matching may be between columns or rows.

Example 1

Yes or No

Fill in a bubble for each part.

For numbers 1a–1d, choose Yes or No to tell whether the number is 3,000 when it is rounded to the nearest thousand.

1a.	3,235	○ Yes	○ No
1b.	3,514	○ Yes	○ No
1c.	3,921	○ Yes	○ No
1d.	2,847	○ Yes	○ No

Example 2

More Than One Correct Choice

Fill in the bubble next to all the correct answers.

Select the equations that show the Commutative Property of Addition. Mark all that apply.

Ⓐ $35 + 56 = 30 + 5 + 50 + 6$

Ⓑ $47 + 68 = 68 + 47$

Ⓒ $32 + 54 = 54 + 32$

Ⓓ $12 + 90 = 90 + 12$

Ⓔ $346 + 932 = 900 + 346 + 32$

Ⓕ $45 + 167 = 40 + 167 + 5$

Example 3

Choose From a List

Circle the word that completes the sentence.

$(25 + 17) + 23 = 25 + (17 + 23)$

The equation shows the addends in a different

order.
grouping.
operation.

Example 4

Sorting

Copy the numbers in the correct box.

Write each number in the box below the word that describes it.

| 33 | 46 | 72 | 97 |

Even	Odd

Example 5

Use Given Numbers in the Answer

Write the given numbers to answer the question.

Write the numbers in order from least to greatest.

| 345 | 267 | 390 | 714 | 873 |

_____   _____   _____   _____   _____

Example 6

Matching

Draw lines to match an item in one column to the related item in the other column.

Match the pairs of related facts.

$8 + 7 = 15$ •   • $12 - 9 = 3$

$14 - 8 = 6$ •   • $7 + 8 = 15$

$3 + 9 = 12$ •   • $9 + 7 = 16$

$16 - 7 = 9$ •   • $14 - 6 = 8$

Name _____

Practice Test
3.OA.1
Represent and solve problems
involving multiplication and division.

1. Alondra makes 4 necklaces. She uses 5 beads on each necklace.

   For numbers 1a–1d, choose Yes or No to tell if the number sentence could be used to find the number of beads Alondra uses.

1a.	$4 \times 5 = \blacksquare$	○ Yes	○ No
1b.	$4 + 4 + 4 + 4 = \blacksquare$	○ Yes	○ No
1c.	$5 + 5 + 5 + 5 = \blacksquare$	○ Yes	○ No
1d.	$5 + 4 = \blacksquare$	○ Yes	○ No

2. A waiter carried 6 baskets with 5 dinner rolls in each basket. How many dinner rolls did he carry? Show your work.

   _____ dinner rolls

3. Lucy and her mother made tacos. They put 2 tacos on each of 7 plates.

   Select the number sentences that show all the tacos Lucy and her mother made. Mark all that apply.

   Ⓐ $2 + 2 + 2 + 2 + 2 + 2 + 2 = 14$

   Ⓑ $2 + 7 = 9$

   Ⓒ $7 + 7 = 14$

   Ⓓ $8 + 6 = 14$

   Ⓔ $2 \times 7 = 14$

GO ON ➡

4. A bookcase has 4 shelves. Each shelf holds 5 books. How many books are in the bookcase?

Draw counters to model the problem. Then explain how you solved the problem.

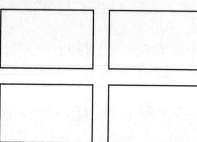

_____

_____

5. Carlos spent 5 minutes working on each of 8 math problems. He can use 8 × 5 to find the total amount of time he spent on the problems.

For numbers 5a–5d, choose Yes or No to show which are equal to 8 × 5.

5a.   8 + 5   ○ Yes   ○ No

5b.   5 + 5 + 5 + 5 + 5   ○ Yes   ○ No

5c.   8 + 8 + 8 + 8 + 8   ○ Yes   ○ No

5d.   5 + 5 + 5 + 5 + 5 + 5 + 5 + 5   ○ Yes   ○ No

6. There are 3 boats on the lake. Six people ride in each boat. How many people ride in the boats? Draw circles to model the problem and explain how to solve it.

_____ people

1. The coach separated the 18 players at lacrosse practice into 3 different groups. How many players were in each group?

_____ players

2. Tyrone took 16 pennies from his bank and put them in 4 equal stacks. How many pennies did Tyrone put in each stack? Show your work.

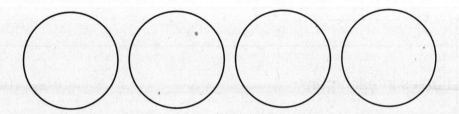

_____ pennies

3. Darius bakes 18 muffins for his friends. He gives each of his friends an equal number of muffins and has none left over.

Part A

Draw a picture to show one way that Darius could have divided the muffins and complete the sentence.

Darius gave muffins to _____ friends.

Part B

Could Darius have divided all of his muffins equally among 4 of his friends? Explain why or why not.

_____

_____

GO ON ➡

4. A workbook is 64 pages long. If each chapter is 8 pages long, how many chapters are there?

_____ chapters

5. Elizabeth has 12 horses on her farm. She puts an equal number of horses in each of 3 pens. How many horses are in each pen?

Circle a number that makes the sentence true.

There are | 4
 9
 36 | horses in each pen.

6. There are 7 cars in an amusement park ride. There are 42 people divided equally among the 7 cars. How many people ride in one car?

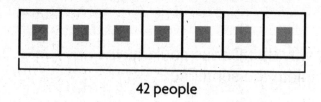

42 people

_____ people

7. There were 40 fingers total on the number of gloves Mrs. Edwards knitted. How many gloves did Mrs. Edwards knit?

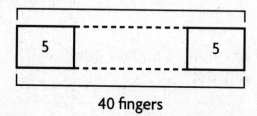

40 fingers

_____ gloves

1. José buys 6 bags of flour. Each bag weighs 5 pounds. How many pounds of flour did José buy?

_____ pounds

2. Use the number line to show the product of 8 × 4.

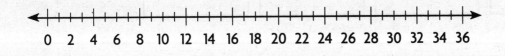

0 2 4 6 8 10 12 14 16 18 20 22 24 26 28 30 32 34 36

8 × 4 = _____

3. Ana used 49 strawberries to make 7 strawberry smoothies. She used the same number of strawberries in each smoothie. How many strawberries did Ana use in each smoothie?

_____ strawberries

4. Chris plants 25 pumpkin seeds in 5 equal rows. How many seeds does Chris plant in each row?

Make an array to represent the problem. Then solve the problem.

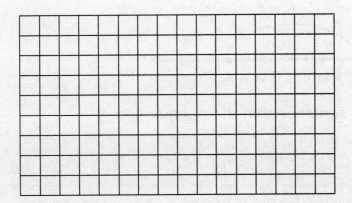

_____ seeds

GO ON ▶

Name _____

5. Mrs. Ruiz sorted spools of thread into 4 boxes. Each box holds 5 spools. How many spools of thread does Mrs. Ruiz have?

Draw circles to model the problem. Then solve. Explain how you solved the problem.

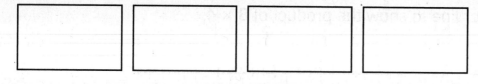

_____

_____

6. Ming divided 35 marbles among 7 different friends. Each friend received the same number of marbles. How many marbles did Ming give to each friend?

$$35 \div 7 = a$$

$$7 \times a = 35$$

(A) 4   (C) 6

(B) 5   (D) 7

7. Lindsay went hiking for two days in Yellowstone National Park. The first jump on the number line shows how many birds she saw the first day. She saw the same number of birds the next day.

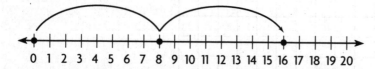

Write the multiplication sentence that the number line shows.

_____ × _____ = _____

1. For numbers 1a–1d, choose Yes or No to show whether the unknown factor is 6.

   1a. $4 \times \blacksquare = 32$ ○ Yes   ○ No

   1b. $\blacksquare \times 6 = 36$ ○ Yes   ○ No

   1c. $8 \times \blacksquare = 49$ ○ Yes   ○ No

   1d. $\blacksquare \times 30 = 180$ ○ Yes   ○ No

2. Devon has 80 books to pack in boxes. She packs 20 books in each box. How many boxes does she need?

   Write an equation using the letter n to stand for the unknown factor. Explain how to find the unknown factor.

   _____

   _____

   _____

3. Circle the unknown factor and quotient.

   $$8 \times \begin{array}{|c|} \hline 6 \\ 7 \\ 8 \\ \hline \end{array} = 48 \qquad \begin{array}{|c|} \hline 6 \\ 7 \\ 8 \\ \hline \end{array} = 48 \div 8$$

4. Keith arranged 40 toy cars in 8 equal rows. How many toy cars are in each row?

   _____ toy cars

GO ON

Name _____

5. The camping club wants to rent rafts. Each raft can hold 8 people. Which equation could be used to find how many rafts are needed for 32 people?

(A) $8 \times 32 = \blacksquare$

(B) $32 \times \blacksquare = 8$

(C) $\blacksquare \times 8 = 32$

(D) $32 \times 8 = \blacksquare$

6. Cody saves all his nickels. Today he is getting them out of his piggy bank and wrapping them to take to the bank. He finds he has 360 nickels. It takes 40 nickels to fill each paper wrapper and make a roll. How many wrappers does he need?

Part A

Write an equation using n for the unknown factor that could be used to find the number of wrappers needed.

_____ $\times$ _____ = _____

Part B

Explain how you solved this problem and how you know your answer is correct.

_____

_____

_____

STOP

Practice Test

COMMON CORE **3.OA.5**
Understand properties of multiplication and the relationship between multiplication and division.

1. Break apart the array to show $8 \times 6 = (4 \times 6) + (4 \times 6)$.

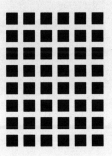

2. Nadia has 4 sheets of stickers. There are 8 stickers on each sheet. She wrote this number sentence to represent the total number of stickers.

$$4 \times 8 = 32$$

What is a related number sentence that also represents the total number of stickers she has?

Ⓐ $8 + 4 = \blacksquare$

Ⓑ $4 + 4 + 4 + 4 = \blacksquare$

Ⓒ $8 \times 8 = \blacksquare$

Ⓓ $8 \times 4 = \blacksquare$

3. Make true equations. Select a number to complete the equation.

0	1	7

$7 \div 7 =$ _____ $7 \div 1 =$ _____ $0 \div 7 =$ _____

GO ON

Name _____

4. Select the number sentences that show the Commutative Property of Multiplication. Mark all that apply.

Ⓐ $3 \times 2 = 2 \times 3$

Ⓑ $4 \times 9 = 4 \times 9$

Ⓒ $5 \times 0 = 0$

Ⓓ $6 \times 1 = 1 \times 6$

Ⓔ $7 \times 2 = 14 \times 1$

5. Circle groups to show $3 \times (2 \times 3)$.

6. For numbers 6a–6d, choose Yes or No to indicate whether the number sentence has the same value as 7×5.

6a. $7 + (3 + 2) = \blacksquare$ ○ Yes   ○ No

6b. $7 \times (3 + 2) = \blacksquare$ ○ Yes   ○ No

6c. $(5 \times 4) + (5 \times 3) = \blacksquare$ ○ Yes   ○ No

6d. $(7 \times 2) + (7 \times 5) = \blacksquare$ ○ Yes   ○ No

STOP

1. Philip has 30 pennies that he exchanges for nickels. He exchanges 5 pennies for each nickel. How many nickels does Philip get?

Ring equal groups to model the problem.

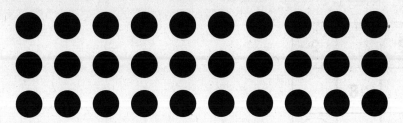

_____ nickels

2. There are 56 apples packed in 7 baskets with the same number of apples in each basket. How many apples are in each basket?

For numbers 2a–2d, choose Yes or No to tell whether the equation represents the problem.

2a. $56 + 7 = \blacksquare$ ○ Yes   ○ No

2b. $7 \times \blacksquare = 56$ ○ Yes   ○ No

2c. $56 \div \blacksquare = 8$ ○ Yes   ○ No

2d. $56 - \blacksquare = 8$ ○ Yes   ○ No

3. There are 35 prizes in 5 equal rows. How many prizes are in each row?

Complete each equation to represent the problem.

$5 \times \underline{\hspace{2cm}} = 35$ $35 \div 5 = \underline{\hspace{2cm}}$

_____ prizes

GO ON ➡

4. Write the numbers that complete the number puzzle.

| 3 | 5 | 8 | 10 | 18 | 24 | 45 |

×	9		2
6		18	
	45	15	◯
	72	24	16

Explain how you found the number in the circle.

5. Circle numbers to complete the related facts.

| 7 |
| 9 |
| 64 |
| 80 |

× 8 = 72   72 ÷

| 7 |
| 8 |
| 9 |
| 64 |

= 8

6. Penn has 12 eggs to use in some recipes. Select a way that he could divide the eggs equally among some recipes. Mark all that apply.

(A) 6 eggs in each of 2 recipes   (D) 4 eggs in each of 4 recipes

(B) 5 eggs in each of 3 recipes   (E) 2 eggs in each of 6 recipes

(C) 3 eggs in each of 4 recipes   (F) 4 eggs in each of 3 recipes

1. Bella made $21 selling bracelets. She wants to know how many bracelets she sold. Bella used this number line.

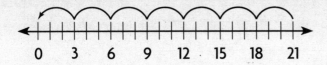

Write the division equation that the number line represents.

_____ ÷ _____ = _____

2. Etta buys some ribbon and cuts it into 7 pieces that are the same length. Each piece is 9 inches long. How long was the ribbon that Etta bought?

_____ inches

3. Complete the chart to show the quotients.

÷	27	36	54	45
9				

4. Use the numbers to write related multiplication and division facts.

_____

_____

GO ON →

5. Each picnic table seats 6 people. How many picnic tables are needed to seat 24 people? Explain the strategy you used to solve the problem.

_____

_____

6. Circle the symbol that makes the multiplication sentence true.

$$9 \times 6 \quad \boxed{\begin{array}{c} > \\ < \\ = \end{array}} \quad 3 \times (3 \times 9)$$

7. Select the equations that represent the array. Mark all that apply.

(A) $3 \times 5 = \blacksquare$

(B) $2 \times \blacksquare = 12$

(C) $\blacksquare \div 3 = 5$

(D) $5 \times \blacksquare = 15$

(E) $12 \div 3 = \blacksquare$

(F) $15 \div 5 = \blacksquare$

8. Write related facts for the array. Explain why there are not more related facts.

_____

_____

Name _____

1. For numbers 1a–1e, select Yes or No to show whether each equation is true.

   1a. $81 \div 9 + 2 = 11$ ○ Yes ○ No

   1b. $6 + 4 \times 5 = 50$ ○ Yes ○ No

   1c. $10 + 10 \div 2 = 15$ ○ Yes ○ No

   1d. $12 - 3 \times 2 = 6$ ○ Yes ○ No

   1e. $20 \div 4 \times 5 = 1$ ○ Yes ○ No

2. Mrs. Garcia puts 57 cans on a shelf. She puts an equal number of cans in each of 9 rows and puts 3 cans in the last row. How many cans does she put in each of the 9 equal rows?

   Choose the equation that can be used to solve the problem.

   I can use the equation
   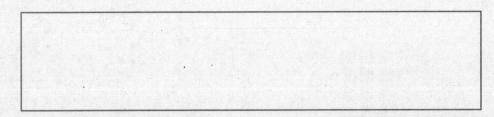
   $(3 \times c) + 9 = 57$

   $(9 \times c) + 3 = 57$

   $(57 \div 9) + 3 = c$

   Solve the problem.

   _____

   _____ cans

GO ON →

3. Bella is planning to write in a journal. Some pages will have one journal entry on them, and other pages will have two journal entries on them. If Bella wants to make 10 entries, how many different ways can she write them in her journal?

4. Brian is going camping in 2 weeks and 2 days.

Which equation can be used to find the number of days until Brian goes camping?

Ⓐ $2 + 7 + 2 = c$; $c = 11$ days

Ⓑ $2 \times 7 - 2 = c$; $c = 12$ days

Ⓒ $2 \times 5 + 2 = c$; $c = 12$ days

Ⓓ $2 \times 7 + 2 = c$; $c = 16$ days

5. Eleni bought 3 packs of crayons. She then found 3 crayons in her desk. Eleni now has 24 crayons. How many crayons were in each pack she bought? Explain how you solved the problem.

_____

_____

Name _____

1. Tim says the rule for the pattern shown in the table is "Add 3." Is his rule correct? Explain how you know.

Packages	1	2	3	4	5
Markers	4	8	12	16	20

_____

_____

_____

2. Select the number sentences that show the Commutative Property of Addition. Mark all that apply.

Ⓐ $14 + 8 = 22$

Ⓑ $8 + 14 = 14 + 8$

Ⓒ $8 + (13 + 1) = (8 + 13) + 1$

Ⓓ $5 + 9 + 8 = 9 + 5 + 8$

3. Heather's puppy weighs 23 pounds. He has been gaining 3 pounds every month as he grows. If this pattern continues, how much will the puppy weigh 5 months from now?

_____

4. Helene selected an odd number to be multiplied by the factors in this table. Write *even* or *odd* to describe each product.

×	1	2	3	4	5
odd number					

GO ON

Name _____

5. Chloe bought 4 movie tickets. Each ticket cost $6. What was the total cost of the movie tickets?

$ _____

6. Complete the table. Amir said a rule for the pattern shown in this table is "Multiply by 4." Is he correct? Explain how you know your answer is reasonable.

Cans	2	3	4		6
Peaches	8	12		20	

_____

_____

7. Lisa completed the table to describe the product of a mystery one-digit number and each factor in the table.

×	1	2	3	4	5
?	even	even	even	even	even

Part A

Give all of the possible numbers that could be Lisa's mystery one-digit number.

_____

Part B

Explain how you know that you have selected all of the correct possibilities.

_____

_____

_____

Name _____

Practice Test

COMMON CORE **3.NBT.1**
Use place value understanding and properties of operations to perform multi-digit arithmetic.

1. There are 486 books in the classroom library. Complete the chart to show 486 rounded to the nearest 10.

Hundreds	Tens	Ones

2. Write each number sentence in the box below the better estimate of the sum.

   393 + 225 = ▭   481 + 215 = ▭

   352 + 328 = ▭   309 + 335 = ▭

600	700

3. Select the numbers that round to 300 when rounded to the nearest hundred. Mark all that apply.

   (A) 238

   (B) 250

   (C) 283

   (D) 342

   (E) 359

4. A total of 907 people went to a fishing tournament. Of these people, 626 arrived before noon. Alina estimates that fewer than 300 people arrived in the afternoon. How did she estimate? Explain.

   _____

   _____

   _____

GO ON

Name _____

5. Select the numbers that round to 100. Select all that apply.

(A) 38   (C) 109

(B) 162   (D) 83

6. Alex and Erika collect shells. The tables show the kinds of shells they collected.

Alex's Shells	
Shell	**Number of Shells**
Scallop	36
Jingle	95
Clam	115

Erika's Shells	
Shell	**Number of Shells**
Scallop	82
Clam	108
Whelk	28

Part A

Who collected more shells? About how many more did she collect? Explain how you solved the problem.

Part B

Alex and Erika have the greatest number of what kind of shell? How many shells of that kind do they have in all? Show your work.

Name _____

Practice Test

3.NBT.2
Use place value understanding
and properties of operations to perform
multi-digit arithmetic.

1. Daniel has 402 pieces in a building set. He uses
   186 pieces to build a house. How many pieces
   does he have left? Show your work.

Use the table for 2–4.

Susie's Sweater Shop	
Month	**Number of Sweaters Sold**
January	402
February	298
March	171

2. The table shows the number of sweaters sold online in
   three months. How many sweaters were sold in January
   and February?

   _____ sweaters

3. How many more sweaters were sold in January
   than March?

   _____ sweaters

4. How many more sweaters were sold in February and
   March than in January?

   _____ sweaters

GO ON ➡

Name _____

5. Janna buys 2 bags of dog food for her dogs. One bag weighs 37 pounds. The other bag weighs 15 pounds. How many pounds do both bags weigh? Explain how you solved the problem.

```




```

6. Choose the property that makes the statement true.

The | Identity / Commutative / Associative | Property of addition states that

you can group addends in different ways and get the same sum.

7. Alexandra has 78 emails in her inbox. She deletes 47 emails. How many emails are left in her inbox? Draw jumps and label the number line to show your thinking.

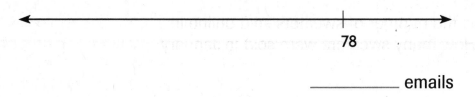

78

_____ emails

8. Luke solves this problem. He says the difference is 214. Explain the mistake Luke made. What is the correct difference?

$352 - 148 =$ _____

```




```

STOP

1. Select the equations that show the Distributive Property. Mark all that apply.

Ⓐ $\quad 8 \times 20 = 8 \times (10 + 10)$

Ⓑ $\quad 5 \times 60 = 5 \times (20 + 40)$

Ⓒ $\quad 30 \times 6 = 6 \times 30$

Ⓓ $\quad 9 \times (4 + 3) = 9 \times 7$

2. The bookstore has 6 shelves of books about animals. There are 30 books on each shelf. How many books about animals does the bookstore have?

Make a diagram to show how you can use the Distributive Property to find the number of books about animals in the bookstore.

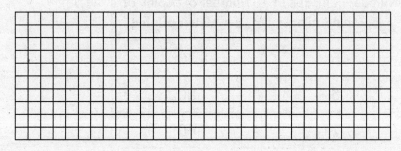

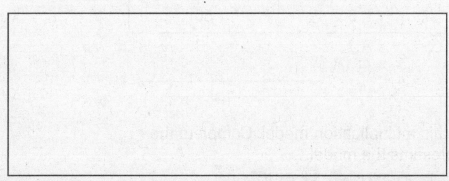

_____ animal books

GO ON

3. Each train can carry 20 cars. Use the number line to find how many cars 6 trains can carry.

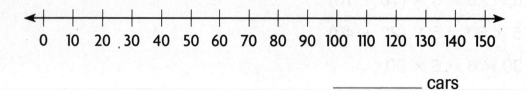

0 10 20 30 40 50 60 70 80 90 100 110 120 130 140 150

_____ cars

4. A store has 30 boxes of melons. Each box holds 4 bags. Each bag holds 2 melons. What is the total number of melons in the store?

_____ melons

5. A printer prints newsletters for many groups every month. Which group uses the greatest number of pieces of paper?

Group	Number of pieces of paper in newsletter	Number of copies of newsletter printed
Garden Ladies	5	70
Book Lovers Club	6	80
Model Train Fans	7	60
Travel Club	8	50

_____

6. Samantha made this multiplication model. Complete the equation that represents the model.

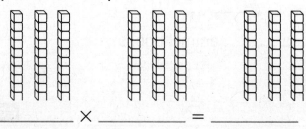

_____ × _____ = _____

1. What fraction names the shaded part? Explain how you know how to write the fraction.

_____

_____

2. Select a numerator and a denominator for the fraction that names the shaded part of the shape.

Numerator	Denominator
○ 2	○ 3
○ 3	○ 5
○ 5	○ 6
○ 6	○ 8

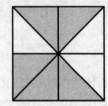

3. Omar shaded a model to show the part of the lawn that he finished mowing. What fraction names the shaded part? Explain how you know how to write the fraction.

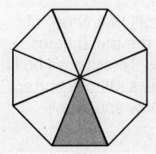

_____

_____

GO ON

Name _____

4. The model shows one whole. What fraction of the model is NOT shaded?

_____

5. Gary paints some shapes.

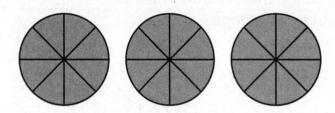

Select one number from each column to show a fraction greater than 1 that names the parts Gary painted.

Numerator	Denominator
○ 3	○ 3
○ 4	○ 4
○ 8	○ 8
○ 24	○ 24

6. Angelo rode his bike around a bike trail that was $\frac{1}{4}$ of a mile long. He rode his bike around the trail 8 times. Angelo says he rode a total of $\frac{8}{4}$ miles. Teresa says he is wrong and that he actually rode 2 miles. Who is correct? Use words and drawings to explain how you know.

_____

_____

_____

_____

Name _____

1. What fraction names point *A* on the number line?

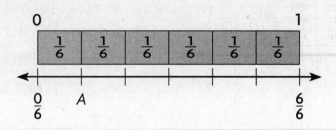

_____

2. Locate and draw point *F* on the number line to represent the fraction $\frac{2}{4}$.

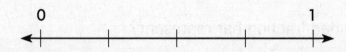

3. Use a straightedge to divide the fraction bar into 6 equal parts. Then shade 4 parts.

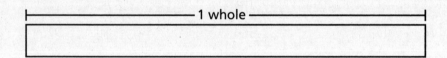

What fraction does the shaded fraction bar represent?

_____

Show the fraction as the sum of unit fractions.

_____

GO ON

4. What fraction names point *A* on the number line?

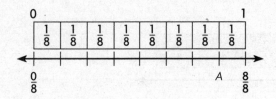

5. Use a straightedge to divide the fraction bar into 4 equal parts. Then shade 3 parts.

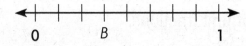

What fraction does the shaded fraction bar represent?

_____

Show the fraction as the sum of unit fractions.

_____

6. Maria drew a number line divided into 8 equal parts. What fraction names point *B* on the number line?

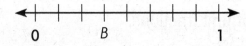

_____

STOP

1. Mrs. Reed baked four pans of lasagna for a family party. Use the rectangles to represent the pans.

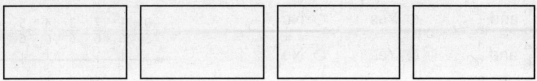

Part A

Draw lines to show how Mrs. Reed could cut one pan of lasagna into thirds, one into fourths, one into sixths, and one into eighths.

Part B

At the end of the dinner, 2 of the pans had $\frac{1}{3}$ of a lasagna left, and 2 of the pans had $\frac{1}{2}$ of a lasagna left. Use the models to show the lasagna that might have been left over in each pan. Write two pairs of equivalent fractions to represent the models.

_____

2. Danielle drew a model to show equivalent fractions.

Use the model to complete the number sentence.

$\frac{1}{2} =$ _____ $=$ _____

3. Sam went for a ride on a sailboat. The ride lasted $\frac{3}{4}$ hour.

What fraction is equivalent to $\frac{3}{4}$?

_____

GO ON ➡

Name _____

4. For numbers 4a–4d, select Yes or No to show whether the fractions are equivalent.

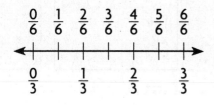

4a. $\frac{6}{6}$ and $\frac{3}{3}$ ○ Yes   ○ No

4b. $\frac{4}{6}$ and $\frac{1}{3}$ ○ Yes   ○ No

4c. $\frac{2}{3}$ and $\frac{3}{6}$ ○ Yes   ○ No

4d. $\frac{1}{3}$ and $\frac{2}{6}$ ○ Yes   ○ No

5. Mr. Worth opened new jars of 4 different colors of paint for an art project. All of the jars were the same size.

Part A

Draw lines to show how Mr. Worth could divide one jar of paint into halves, one into thirds, one into fourths, and one into sixths.

Part B

Students in his class used an equivalent amount of paint from the jars divided into halves and fourths. They also used an equivalent amount of paint from the jars divided into thirds and sixths. Use the models to show the amount of paints used. Write two pairs of equivalent fractions to represent the models.

_____

Practice Test
3.NF.3b
Develop understanding of fractions as numbers.

1. There are 12 people having lunch. Each person wants $\frac{1}{3}$ of a sub sandwich. How many whole sub sandwiches are needed? Use the models to show your answer.

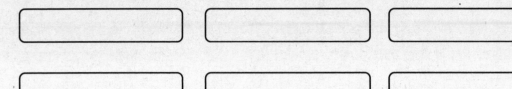

_____ sub sandwiches

2. Tom rode his horse for $\frac{4}{6}$ mile. Liz rode her horse for an equal distance. What is an equivalent fraction that describes how far Liz rode? Use the models to show your work.

3. Mr. Peters made a pizza. There is $\frac{4}{8}$ of the pizza left over. Select the fractions that are equivalent to the part of the pizza that is left over. Mark all that apply.

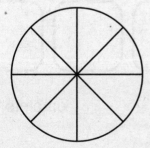

Ⓐ $\frac{5}{8}$ Ⓑ $\frac{3}{4}$ Ⓒ $\frac{2}{4}$ Ⓓ $\frac{1}{2}$

4. Select the fraction that would be included in an equivalence chain for $\frac{1}{4}$. Mark all that apply.

Ⓐ $\frac{4}{4}$

Ⓑ $\frac{2}{8}$

Ⓒ $\frac{1}{6}$

Ⓓ $\frac{6}{2}$

Ⓔ $\frac{3}{12}$

5. Draw a line to match the fraction on the left to an equivalent fraction or number on the right.

$\frac{3}{3}$ •   • $\frac{3}{4}$

$\frac{1}{2}$ •   • 4

$\frac{6}{8}$ •   • $\frac{3}{9}$

$\frac{4}{1}$ •   • 1

$\frac{1}{3}$ •   • $\frac{4}{8}$

6. There are 8 people having breakfast. Each person wants $\frac{1}{2}$ of an omelet. How many whole omelets are needed? Use the models to show your answer.

_____ omelets

STOP

Name _____

1. Use the fractions to label each point on the number line.

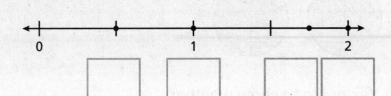

$\frac{1}{2}$ $\frac{9}{3}$

$\frac{5}{5}$ $\frac{10}{5}$

$\frac{1}{3}$ $\frac{7}{4}$

2. Tara ran 3 laps around her neighborhood for a total of 1 mile yesterday. Today she wants to run $\frac{2}{3}$ of a mile. How many laps will she need to run around her neighborhood?

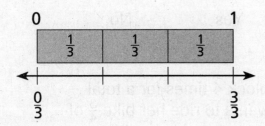

_____ laps

3. Each shape is 1 whole. Which numbers name the parts that are shaded? Mark all that apply.

Ⓐ 4

Ⓑ 6

Ⓒ $\frac{26}{6}$

Ⓓ $\frac{24}{6}$

Ⓔ $\frac{6}{4}$

GO ON ▶

Name _____

4. Each shape is 1 whole.

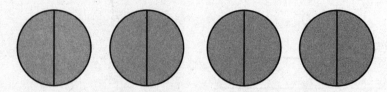

For numbers 4a–4e, choose Yes or No to show whether the number names the parts that are shaded.

4a. 4   ○ Yes   ○ No

4b. 8   ○ Yes   ○ No

4c. $\frac{8}{2}$ ○ Yes   ○ No

4d. $\frac{8}{4}$ ○ Yes   ○ No

4e. $\frac{2}{8}$ ○ Yes   ○ No

5. Lucy rode her bike around the block 4 times for a total of 1 mile yesterday. Today she wants to ride her bike $\frac{3}{4}$ of a mile. How many times will she need to ride her bike around the block?

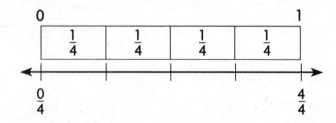

_____ times

6. Henry and Reiko both use 1 yard of ribbon to make bows. Write two different fractions to show that Henry and Reiko use the same amount of ribbon.

Henry uses _____ yard.

Reiko uses _____ yard.

STOP

1. Dan and Miguel are working on the same homework assignment. Dan has finished $\frac{1}{4}$ of the assignment. Miguel has finished $\frac{3}{4}$ of the assignment. Which statement is correct? Mark all that apply.

   (A) Miguel has completed the entire assignment.

   (B) Dan has not completed the entire assignment.

   (C) Miguel has finished more of the assignment than Dan.

   (D) Dan and Miguel have completed equal parts of the assignment.

2. Jenna painted $\frac{1}{8}$ of one side of a fence. Mark painted $\frac{1}{6}$ of the other side of the same fence. Use >, =, or < to compare the parts that they painted.

   _____

3. Chun lives $\frac{3}{8}$ mile from school. Gail lives $\frac{5}{8}$ mile from school.

   Use the fractions and symbols to show which distance is longer.

   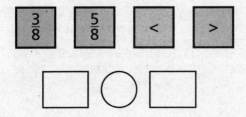

4. Pat has three pieces of fabric that measure $\frac{3}{6}$, $\frac{5}{6}$, and $\frac{2}{6}$ yards long. Write the lengths in order from least to greatest.

   _____

GO ON

Name _____

5. Bill used $\frac{1}{3}$ cup of raisins and $\frac{2}{3}$ cup of banana chips to make a snack.

For numbers 5a–5d, select Yes or No to show whether each comparison is true.

5a. $\frac{1}{3} > \frac{2}{3}$ ○ Yes   ○ No

5b. $\frac{2}{3} = \frac{1}{3}$ ○ Yes   ○ No

5c. $\frac{1}{3} < \frac{2}{3}$ ○ Yes   ○ No

5d. $\frac{2}{3} > \frac{1}{3}$ ○ Yes   ○ No

6. Cora measures the heights of three plants. Draw a line to match each height to the word that describes its place in the order of heights.

$\frac{4}{6}$ foot •   • least

$\frac{4}{4}$ foot •   • between

$\frac{4}{8}$ foot •   • greatest

7. Mavis mixed $\frac{2}{4}$ quart of apple juice with $\frac{1}{2}$ quart of cranberry juice. Compare the fractions. Choose the symbol that makes the statement true.

$$\frac{2}{4} \;\begin{array}{c} < \\ = \\ > \end{array}\; \frac{1}{2}$$

8. Todd and Lisa are comparing fraction strips. Which statements are correct? Mark all that apply.

Ⓐ $\frac{1}{4} < \frac{4}{4}$ Ⓑ $\frac{5}{6} < \frac{4}{6}$ Ⓒ $\frac{2}{3} > \frac{1}{3}$ Ⓓ $\frac{5}{8} > \frac{4}{8}$

Practice Test

3.MD.1
Solve problems involving measurement and estimation of intervals of time, liquid volumes, and masses of objects.

1. Tran checked the time on his watch after he finished his daily run.

Select the time that Tran finished running. Mark all that apply.

(A) 14 minutes before nine   (C) quarter to nine

(B) eight forty-six   (D) nine forty-six

2. Rita's class begins social studies at ten minutes before one in the afternoon. At what time does Rita's class begin social studies? Circle a time that makes the sentence true.

Rita's class begins social studies at

1:10 A.M.
1:10 P.M.
12:50 A.M.
12:50 P.M.

3. Yul and Sarah's art class started at 11:25 A.M. The class lasted 30 minutes. Yul left when the class was done. Sarah stayed an extra 5 minutes to talk with the teacher and then left.

Write the time that each student left. Explain how you found each time.

_____

_____

GO ON

Name _____

4. Anthony's family went out to dinner. They left at the time shown on the clock. They returned home at 6:52 P.M.

Part A

How long was Anthony's family gone?

_____ hour _____ minutes

Part B

Explain how you found your answer.

_____

_____

_____

_____

5. A chicken dish needs to bake in the oven for 35 minutes. The dish needs to cool for at least 8 minutes before serving. Scott puts the chicken dish in the oven at 5:14 P.M.

For numbers 5a–5d, select Yes or No to show whether each statement is true.

5a. Scott can serve the
     dish at 5:51 P.M.   ○ Yes   ○ No

5b. Scott can serve the
     dish at 5:58 P.M.   ○ Yes   ○ No

5c. Scott should take the
     dish out of the oven
     at 5:51 A.M.   ○ Yes   ○ No

5d. Scott should take the
     dish out of the oven
     at 5:49 P.M.   ○ Yes   ○ No

Practice Test

COMMON CORE **3.MD.2**
Solve problems involving measurement and estimation of intervals of time, liquid volumes, and masses of objects.

1. A large bottle of water holds about 2 liters.

For numbers 1a–1e, choose Yes or No to tell whether the container will hold all of the water.

1a. kitchen sink   ○ Yes   ○ No

1b. water glass   ○ Yes   ○ No

1c. ice cube tray   ○ Yes   ○ No

1d. large soup pot   ○ Yes   ○ No

1e. lunchbox thermos   ○ Yes   ○ No

2. Cara uses a balance scale to compare mass.

Circle a symbol that makes the comparison true.

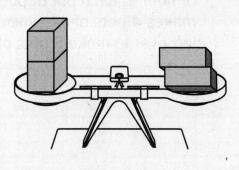

The mass of the blocks the mass of the erasers.

$<$

$>$

$=$

3. Select the items that would be best measured in grams. Mark all that apply.

Ⓐ watermelon

Ⓑ lettuce leaf

Ⓒ grape

Ⓓ onion

GO ON ➡

Name _____

4. Lucy fills a bathroom sink with water. Is the amount of water *more than 1 liter, about 1 liter, or less than 1 liter?* Explain how you know.

_____

_____

_____

5. Amy has 30 grams of flour. She puts 4 grams of flour in each pot of chowder that she makes. She puts 5 grams of flour in each pot of potato soup that she makes. She makes 4 pots of chowder. Does Amy have enough flour left over to make 3 pots of potato soup?

6. A deli makes its own salad dressing. A small jar has 3 grams of spices. A large jar has 5 grams of spices. Will 25 grams of spices be enough to make 3 small jars and 3 large jars? Show your work.

7. Select the objects with a mass greater than 1 kilogram. Mark all that apply.

(A) bicycle

(B) pen

(C) eraser

(D) math book

Name _____

Use the frequency table for 1–2.

1. The Pet Shop keeps track of the number of fish it has for sale. The frequency table shows how many fish are in three tanks.

Fish in Tanks	
Tank	**Number of Fish**
Tank 1	16
Tank 2	9
Tank 3	12

Part A

Use the data in the table to complete the picture graph.

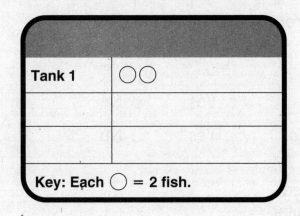

Part B

How many pictures did you draw for Tank 2? Explain.

2. Each tank can hold up to 20 fish. How many more fish can the Pet Shop put in the 3 tanks?

(A) 60 fish

(C) 20 fish

(B) 23 fish

(D) 33 fish

Name _____

Use the bar graph for 3–6.

3. Three more students play piano than which other instrument?

_____

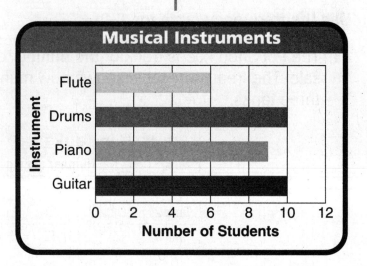

4. The same number of students play which two instruments?

_____

5. For numbers 5a–5d, select Yes or No to show whether each statement is true.

5a. Ten more students play guitar than play flute. ○ Yes   ○ No

5b. Nine students play piano. ○ Yes   ○ No

5c. Six fewer students play flute and piano combined than play drums and guitar combined. ○ Yes   ○ No

5d. Nine more students play piano and guitar combined than play drums. ○ Yes   ○ No

6. There are more students who play the trumpet than play the flute, but fewer students than play the guitar. Explain how you would change the bar graph to show students who play the trumpet.

Use the line plot for 1–2.

Robin collected shells during her vacation. She measured the length of each shell to the nearest inch and recorded the data in a line plot.

```
        X
        X
  X     X           X
  X  X  X           X
  X  X  X  X  X
  +--+--+--+--+--
  5  6  7  8  9
```
Length of Shells in Inches

1. How many shells were 6 inches long or longer?

   _____ shells

2. How many more shells did Robin collect that were 5 inches long than were 8 inches long?

   _____ shells

3. Use an inch ruler to measure.

   Part A

   What is the length of the leaf to the nearest fourth-inch?

   _____ inches

   Part B

   Explain what happens if you line up the left side of the object with the 1 on the ruler.

   _____

   _____

GO ON ➡

Name _____

4. Ashley measures the shells she collects. She records the measurements in a chart.

Number of Shells	Length in Inches
1	1
2	$2\frac{1}{2}$
3	$1\frac{1}{2}$
1	2

Part A

Ashley found a razor clam shell as long as this strip. Use an inch ruler to measure. Record the measurement in the chart.

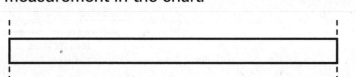

_____ inches

Part B

Complete the line plot to show the data in the chart. How many shells are longer than 2 inches? Tell how you know.

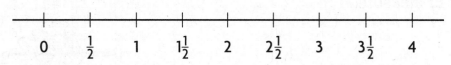

Length of Shells Measured to the Nearest Half Inch

_____

_____

5. Estimate the length of the fork in inches. Then measure it to the nearest $\frac{1}{4}$ inch.

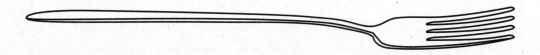

Estimate: _____ in.   Actual: _____ in.

Practice Test
3.MD.5a, 3.MD.5b
Geometric measurement: understand concepts of area and relate area to multiplication and division.

1. Draw a line from the figure to the area of the figure.

•   • 13 square units

•   • 14 square units

•   • 15 square units

2. What is the perimeter and area of this figure?
Explain how you found the answer.

Perimeter _____ units

Area _____ square units

_____

_____

_____

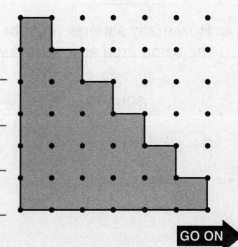

GO ON

Name _____

3. Draw a line from the figure to the area of the figure.

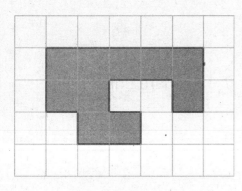

•   • 10 square units

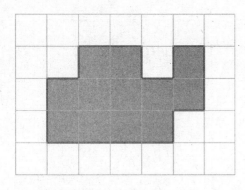

•   • 11 square units

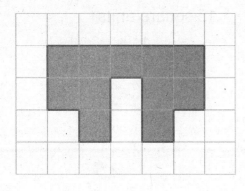

•   • 12 square units

4. How many squares need to be added to this figure so that it has the same area as a square with a side length of 5 units?

_____ squares

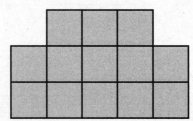

Practice Test
COMMON CORE **3.MD.6**
*Geometric measurement: understand
concepts of area and relate area to
multiplication and division.*

1. What is the area of the figure shown? Each unit square is
1 square meter.

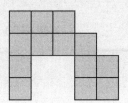

_____ square meters

2. Steve makes a banner with an area of 8 square feet. On a
grid, draw all possible rectangles with an area of 8 square
feet and sides whose lengths are whole feet. Label the
lengths of two adjacent sides of each rectangle. Label
each rectangle with its perimeter.

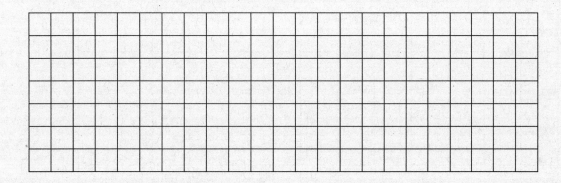

Compare the perimeters of the banners. What do you
notice about their shapes?

GO ON →

Name _____

3. What is the area of the figure shown? Each unit square is 1 square foot.

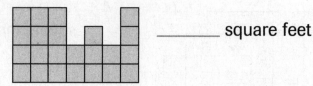

_____ square feet

4. Dory designs a sticker with a perimeter of 14 centimeters. On the grid, draw all possible rectangles with a perimeter of 14 centimeters and sides whose lengths are whole centimeters. Label the lengths of two adjacent sides of each rectangle. Label each rectangle with its area.

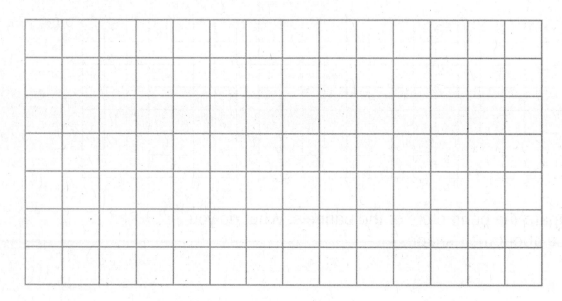

Compare the areas of the rectangles. What do you notice about their shapes?

Name _____

1. Brady is placing square tiles on the floor of the kitchen. Each unit square is 1 square foot.

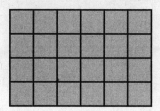

Which equations can Brady use to find the area of the kitchen floor? Mark all that apply.

(A) $4 \times 6 = 24$ (D) $6 + 6 + 6 + 6 = 24$

(B) $4 + 4 + 4 + 4 + 4 = 20$ (E) $4 \times 5 = 20$

(C) $4 + 6 + 4 + 6 = 20$ (F) $6 \times 4 = 24$

2. Simon draws a sketch of the floor of his tree house on grid paper. Each unit square is 1 square foot. Write and solve a multiplication equation that can be used to find the area of the floor in square feet.

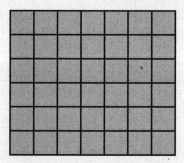

_____

_____ square feet

GO ON

Name _____

3. The drawing shows Seth's plan for a fort in his backyard. Each unit square is 1 square foot.

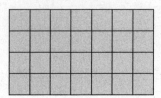

   Which equations can Seth use to find the area of the fort? Mark all that apply.

   (A) $4 + 4 + 4 + 4 = 16$　　　(D) $4 \times 4 = 16$

   (B) $7 + 4 + 7 + 4 = 22$　　　(E) $7 \times 7 = 49$

   (C) $7 + 7 + 7 + 7 = 28$　　　(F) $4 \times 7 = 28$

4. Keisha draws a sketch of her living room on grid paper. Each unit square is 1 square meter. Write and solve a multiplication equation that can be used to find the area of the living room in square meters.

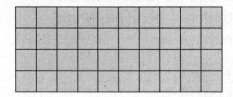

   _____

   _____ square meters

5. Colleen drew this rectangle. Select the equation that can be used to find the area of the rectangle. Mark all that apply.

   (A) 　　　　　$9 \times 6 = n$

   (B) $9 + 9 + 9 + 9 + 9 = n$

   (C) 　　　　　$9 + 6 = n$

   (D) 　　　　　$6 \times 9 = n$

   (E) $6 + 6 + 6 + 6 + 6 = n$

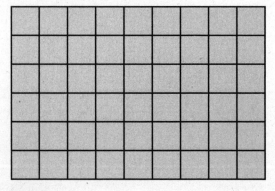

Name _____

Practice Test

3.MD.7b
Geometric measurement: understand
concepts of area and relate area to
multiplication and division.

1. Elizabeth has two rectangular gardens in her yard. The first garden has a length of 8 feet and a width of 6 feet. The second garden is half the length of the first garden. The area of the second garden is twice the area of the first garden. For numbers 1a–1d, select Yes or No to show whether each statement is true.

1a. The area of the first garden
is 48 square feet.   ○ Yes   ○ No

1b. The area of the second
garden is 24 square feet.   ○ Yes   ○ No

1c. The width of the second
garden is 12 feet.   ○ Yes   ○ No

1d. The width of the second
garden is 24 feet.   ○ Yes   ○ No

2. Raul makes a sign for the school fair. It has a length of 9 inches and a width of 8 inches. What is the area of the sign?

Draw a rectangle to help solve the problem. Label your drawing.

Write an equation to solve the problem.

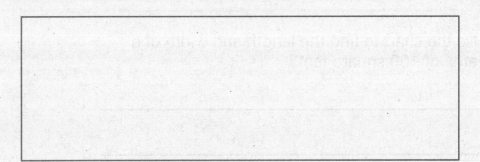

Area of the sign: _____ square inches

GO ON

Name _____

3. Etta prints a photograph that is 7 inches long and 5 inches wide. What is the area of the photograph?

Draw a rectangle to help solve the problem. Label your drawing. Write an equation to solve the problem.

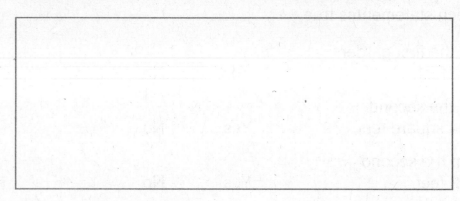

Area of the photograph: _____ square inches

4. Find the pattern and complete the chart.

Total Area (in square feet)	50	60	70	80	
Length (in feet)	10	10		10	
Width (in feet)	5	6	7		

How can you use the chart to find the length and width of a figure with an area of 100 square feet?

_____

_____

STOP

1. Sydney wants to find the area of the large rectangle by adding the areas of the two small rectangles.

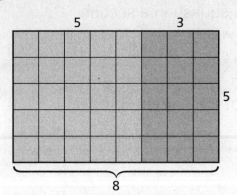

For numbers 1a–1c, choose Yes or No to tell whether or not Sydney could use the expression to find the area of the large rectangle.

1a. $(8 \times 5) + (5 \times 5)$ ○ Yes   ○ No

1b. $25 + 15$ ○ Yes   ○ No

1c. $(5 \times 5) + (3 \times 5)$ ○ Yes   ○ No

2. Kylie wants to find the area of the large rectangle by adding the areas of the two small rectangles.

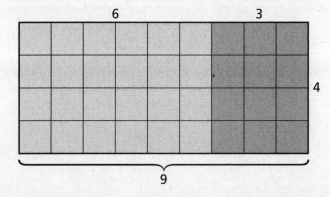

For numbers 2a–2c, choose Yes or No to tell whether or not Kylie could use the expression to find the area of the large rectangle.

2a. $24 + 12$ ○ Yes   ○ No

2b. $(4 \times 6) + (4 \times 3)$ ○ Yes   ○ No

2c. $(6 \times 4) + (9 \times 4)$ ○ Yes   ○ No

GO ON

Name _____

3. Liana plants a vegetable garden in two rectangular
sections. She plants corn in a section that is 5 meters
long and 6 meters wide. She plants squash in a section
that is 3 meters long and 6 meters wide.

Part A

Describe one way to find the area of the garden. Then
find the area.

Area: _____ square meters

Part B

Draw a picture of the garden to show your answer is
correct.

Name _____

Practice Test

3.MD.7d
Geometric measurement: understand
concepts of area and relate area to
multiplication and division.

1. Mrs. Rios puts tape around the section of wall shown to indicate the area of the mural she will paint.

   What is the area of the section she wants to paint? Show your work.

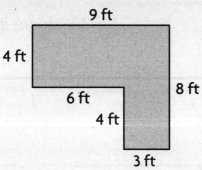

   _____ square feet

2. Draw a line from the figure to the area of the figure.

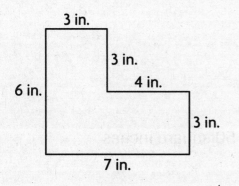

   •   • 44 square inches

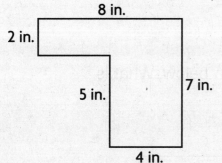

   •   • 30 square inches

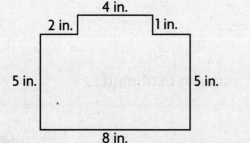

   •   • 36 square inches

Name _____

3. Draw a line from the figure to the area of the figure.

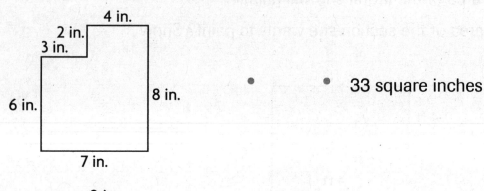

●   ● 33 square inches

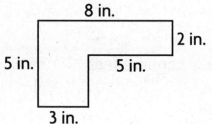

●   ● 25 square inches

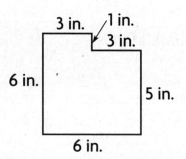

●   ● 50 square inches

4. Kendra used markers to color the shape shown below. What is the area of the shape? Show your work.

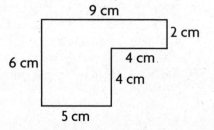

_____ square centimeters

STOP

Name _____

Practice Test

3.MD.8
Geometric measurement: recognize perimeter as an attribute of plane figures and distinguish between linear and area measures.

1. Kim wants to put trim around a picture she drew. How many centimeters of trim does Kim need for the perimeter of the picture?

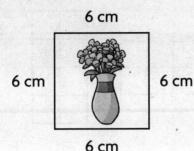

6 cm

6 cm   6 cm

6 cm

_____ centimeters

2. Yuji drew this figure on grid paper. What is the perimeter of the figure?

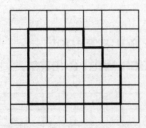

_____ units

3. Shawn drew a rectangle that was 2 units wide and 6 units long. Draw a different rectangle that has the same perimeter but a different area.

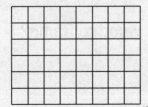

GO ON

4. Which figure has a perimeter of 20 units and an area of 16 square units?

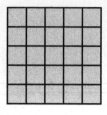 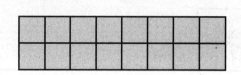 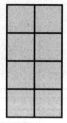 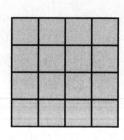

(A)   (B)   (C)   (D)

5. Anthony wants to make two different rectangular flowerbeds, each with an area of 24 square feet. He will build a wooden frame around each flowerbed. The flowerbeds will have side lengths that are whole numbers.

Part A

Each unit square on the grid below is 1 square foot. Draw two possible flowerbeds. Label each with a letter.

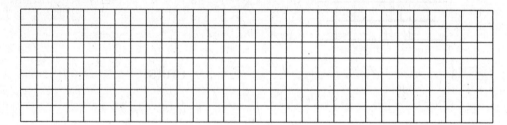

Part B

Which of the flowerbeds will take more wood to frame? Explain how you know.

_____

_____

_____

1. Which words describe this shape? Mark all that apply.

  Ⓐ polygon

  Ⓑ open shape

  Ⓒ pentagon

  Ⓓ quadrilateral

2. Which words describe this shape? Mark all that apply.

rectangle	rhombus	quadrilateral	square
Ⓐ	Ⓑ	Ⓒ	Ⓓ

3. Write the name of each triangle where it belongs in the table. Some triangles might belong in both parts of the table. Some triangles might not belong in either part.

Has 1 Right Angle	Has at Least 2 Sides of Equal Length

Name _____

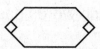

4. Circle a number or word from each box to complete the sentence to describe this shape.

There are
| 2 |
| 3 |
| 4 |
right angles and
| 2 |
| 3 |
| 4 |
angles
| less |
| greater |
than a right angle.

5. Rhea used a Venn diagram to sort shapes. What label could she use for circle A?

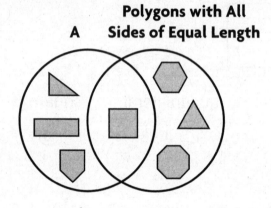

_____

6. Ava drew a quadrilateral with 2 pairs of opposite sides that are parallel. The shape has at least 2 right angles. Draw a shape that Ava could have drawn.

Name _____

1. This hexagon has been divided into triangles with equal areas. What part of the area of the hexagon is the area of each triangle?

(A) $\frac{1}{2}$

(B) $\frac{1}{5}$

(C) $\frac{1}{6}$

(D) $\frac{6}{6}$

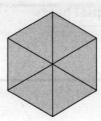

2. Divide each shape into the number of equal parts shown. Then write the fraction that describes each part of the whole.

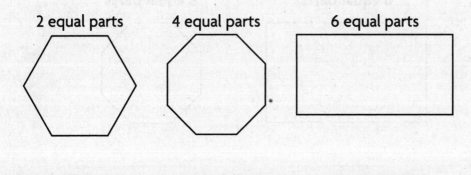

2 equal parts   4 equal parts   6 equal parts

_____   _____   _____

3. Victor drew lines to divide a trapezoid into equal parts that represent $\frac{1}{3}$ of the whole area. Draw lines to show how Victor divided the trapezoid.

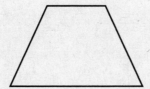

GO ON ▶

Name _____

4. Divide each shape into the number of equal parts shown. Then write the fraction that describes each part of the whole.

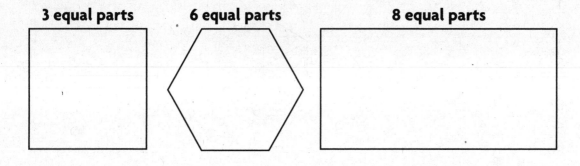

3 equal parts   **6 equal parts**   **8 equal parts**

_____   _____   _____

5. Divide each shape into the number of equal parts shown. Then write the fraction that describes each part of the whole.

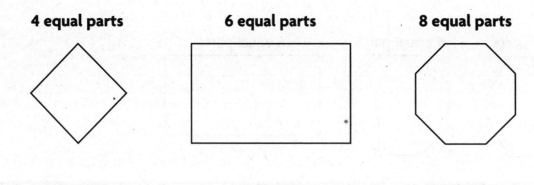

4 equal parts   **6 equal parts**   **8 equal parts**

_____   _____   _____

6. Colette drew lines to divide a rectangle into equal parts that each represent $\frac{1}{4}$ of the whole area. Her first line is shown. Draw to complete Colette's model.

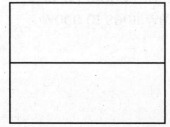

STOP

1. Carly bought 3 equal-sized packs of baseball cards. She gave 5 cards to her sister. Now she has 19 cards. How many baseball cards were in each pack? Explain how you solved the problem.

_____

_____

_____

2. Write each number sentence in the box below the better estimate of the sum.

281 + 125 = ■   202 + 128 = ■

186 + 119 = ■   309 + 135 = ■

300	400

3. Kwan divided this circle into equal parts. Circle the word that makes the sentence true.

The circle is divided into
| sixths |
| eighths |
| fourths |

4. Taylor is building a birdhouse for his backyard. He needs a piece of wood that is 8 inches long and 6 inches wide. What is the area of the piece of wood Taylor needs?

Draw a rectangle to help solve the problem. Label your drawing. Write an equation to solve the problem.

Area of piece of wood: _____ square inches.

5. Hal completed the table to describe the product of a mystery one-digit number and each factor in the table.

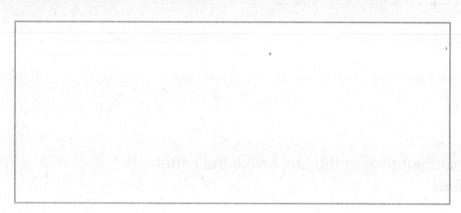

×	1	2	3	4	5
?	odd	even	odd	even	odd

Part A

Give all of the possible numbers that could be Hal's mystery one-digit number.

_____

Part B

Explain how you know that you have selected all of the correct possibilities.

_____

_____

GO ON

6. For items 6a–6d, choose Yes or No to show whether
the unknown factor is 9.

6a. $6 \times \blacksquare = 56$ ○ Yes   ○ No

6b. $\blacksquare \times 4 = 42$ ○ Yes   ○ No

6c. $8 \times \blacksquare = 72$ ○ Yes   ○ No

6d. $\blacksquare \times 50 = 450$ ○ Yes   ○ No

7. Mikio drove 58 miles on Saturday. On Sunday he drove
23 miles. How many miles did he drive on Saturday and
Sunday? Explain how you solved the problem.

8. Three friends are collecting canned
food for the food bank. The picture
graph shows the number of cans each
has collected so far.

Choose the name from each box that
makes the sentence true.

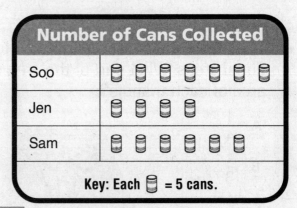

Number of Cans Collected

Key: Each ▯ = 5 cans.

Ten fewer cans were collected by
| Soo |
| Jen |
| Sam |

than
| Soo |
| Jen |
| Sam |
.

GO ON

9. Elian made 36 ounces of punch. He pours the same amount into each of 6 cups. How many ounces of punch does he pour into each cup?

Circle the amount to complete the sentence.

Elian poured
6
9
12
30
 ounces of punch into each cup.

10. Select the number sentences that show the Commutative Property of Multiplication. Mark all that apply.

(A) $5 \times 2 = 5 + 5$

(B) $6 \times 0 = 0$

(C) $7 \times 5 = 5 \times 7$

(D) $8 \times 1 = 1 \times 8$

(E) $9 \times 1 = 9$

11. The trapezoid has been divided into triangles with equal areas. What part of the area of the trapezoid is the area of each triangle?

(A) $\frac{1}{4}$

(B) $\frac{1}{3}$

(C) $\frac{1}{2}$

(D) $\frac{3}{3}$

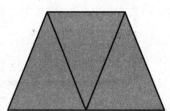

12. A football game begins at 11:32 A.M. The game lasts 3 hours 16 minutes. When does the game end?

_____

GO ON

13. Heidi is placing square tiles on her desk. Each unit square is 1 square inch.

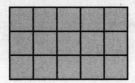

Which equations can Heidi use to find the area of the tiles? Mark all that apply.

(A) $3 + 3 + 3 + 3 = 12$ (D) $5 \times 3 = 15$

(B) $5 + 5 + 5 = 15$ (E) $3 + 3 + 3 + 3 + 3 = 15$

(C) $3 \times 5 = 15$ (F) $3 + 5 + 3 + 5 = 16$

14. There are 4 flower beds in Max's yard. Three rosebushes grow in each flower bed. How many rosebushes are there? Draw circles to model the problem and explain how to solve it.

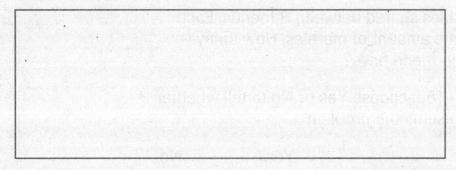

_____ rosebushes

15. What fraction names point *A* on the number line?

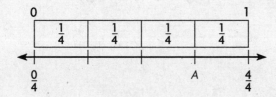

_____

GO ON

16. Pete drew a diagram of his backyard on grid paper. Each unit square is 1 square meter. The area surrounding the patio is grass.

How much more of the backyard is grass than patio? Show your work.

_____ more square meters

17. Select the equations that show the Distributive Property. Mark all that apply.

Ⓐ $3 \times 60 = 3 \times (20 + 20 + 20)$

Ⓑ $5 \times 20 = (5 \times 2) \times (5 \times 10)$

Ⓒ $50 \times 7 = 7 \times 50$

Ⓓ $8 \times 40 = 8 \times (10 + 30)$

18. There are 18 marbles shared between 3 friends. Each friend has the same amount of marbles. How many marbles does each friend have?

For numbers 18a–18d, choose Yes or No to tell whether the equation represents the problem.

18a. $18 \div 3 = \blacksquare$ ○ Yes   ○ No

18b. $18 + 3 = \blacksquare$ ○ Yes   ○ No

18c. $3 \times \blacksquare = 18$ ○ Yes   ○ No

18d. $18 - \blacksquare = 3$ ○ Yes   ○ No

GO ON

19. Each team at a science competition has 6 players. How many teams are there if 42 players are at the competition? Explain the strategy you used to solve the problem.

_____

_____

_____

20. Gina arranges her 21 puzzles in 7 equal stacks. How many puzzles does Gina put in each stack?

Shade squares to make an array to model the problem.

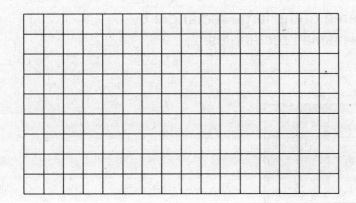

_____ puzzles

21. Which rectangle has the same number of square units for its area as it has units for its perimeter?

Ⓐ 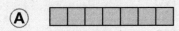   Ⓒ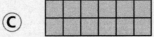

Ⓑ   Ⓓ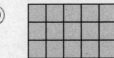

GO ON ➡

22. What is the area of the figure shown? Each unit square is 1 square centimeter.

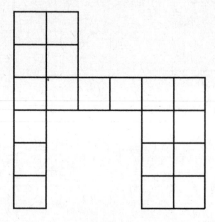

_____ square centimeters

23. Mason wants to find the area of the large rectangle by adding the areas of the two small rectangles.

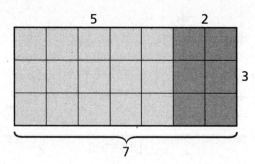

For numbers 23a–23d, choose Yes or No to show whether Mason could use the expression to find the area of the large rectangle.

23a. (5 × 3) + (2 × 3)   ○ Yes   ○ No

23b. (3 × 5) + (3 × 2)   ○ Yes   ○ No

23c. (5 × 3) + (7 × 3)   ○ Yes   ○ No

23d. 15 + 6   ○ Yes   ○ No

GO ON ▶

A Barbecue

**The community center is having a barbecue. Many
people bring food and games to the barbecue. Use your
knowledge of fractions to solve the problems.**

1. Zach's family brings a large sandwich to the barbecue.
   They cut the sandwich into 8 equal parts. Four people
   each take one piece of the sandwich.

   a. Draw a picture to show the sandwich. Shade the parts
   that were eaten.

   b. Write a fraction to show how much of the sandwich
   was eaten.

   _____

   c. Draw another sandwich cut into 4 equal parts. Shade
   the sandwich to show an equivalent fraction to the
   sandwich Zach's family brought to the barbecue.

   d. Then write a pair of equivalent fractions for the
   sandwiches.

   GO ON ➡

2. Mrs. Lin brings 6 trays of hamburger buns to the barbecue. $\frac{2}{3}$ of the trays have wheat buns.

a. How many of the trays have wheat buns? Draw a diagram to solve the problem.

_____ trays

b. Write a pair of equivalent fractions for the diagram that you drew. Explain why the fractions are equivalent.

_____

_____

3. Mr. Sanchez brings a tray of 6 granola bars to the barbecue. The bars are all the same size. Four people share each of the bars equally.

a. Explain how they could divide all the bars so each person gets the same amount. Draw pictures to show your thinking.

_____

_____

_____

b. Suppose the four people only eat 4 equal-size pieces of granola bars. Compare the number of granola bars that were eaten with the number of bars not eaten. Write a fraction sentence. Use <, >, or =.

_____

GO ON

4. William and Cassie bring pies to the barbecue. They cut
them into different parts and serve them.

   a. The table shows the parts of pie people ate. Shade
   each pie to show what was eaten. Then write the
   fraction.

three sixths	four eighths	three fourths

_____   _____   _____

   b. Look at the pies you shaded. Which two show
   equivalent fractions? Write a pair of equivalent
   fractions.

   _____

   c. Which two fractions have the same numerator?
   Compare the fractions. Write a sentence using > or <.

   _____

   _____

   d. Look at the fraction you drew for four eighths. Write
   a fraction that is greater. Write a fraction that is less.
   Then write the fractions in order from least to greatest.

   _____

   _____

   _____

GO ON ➡

5. Milos brings 12 hamburgers to the barbecue. He puts cheese on 4 hamburgers.

   a. Draw to show the fraction. Write two equivalent fractions. Explain why they are equivalent fractions.

_____

_____

_____

   b. Milos says that $\frac{4}{8}$ of the hamburgers have cheese. Explain why Milos is correct or incorrect.

_____

_____

_____

6. There is a track next to the barbecue area. The track is $\frac{1}{4}$ mile long. A group of students have a relay race. They run around the track 4 times.

   a. Draw a number line to show how many miles the students ran. Use 0 and 1 as points on your number line. Divide the number line into equal parts to solve the problem. Then write an equivalent fraction.

_____

   b. Suppose the students ran the track 8 more times. Write a fraction to show how many miles they ran.

_____

1. Kaitlyn says that $8 \div 2 \times 4$ is the same as $4 \times 2 \div 8$.
Is Kaitlyn correct or incorrect? Explain.

_____

_____

_____

_____

2. Write each number sentence in the box below the better estimate of the sum.

$263 + 189 =$ ■ $195 + 238 =$ ■

$215 + 289 =$ ■ $305 + 72 =$ ■

400	500

3. Jamal folded this piece of paper into equal parts.
Circle the word that makes the sentence true.

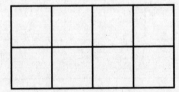

The paper is folded into
sixths

eighths

fourths
.

GO ON ➡

4. Chloe painted a picture that is 9 inches long and 5 inches wide. What is the area of the picture?

Draw a rectangle to help solve the problem. Label your drawing. Write an equation to solve the problem.

Area of the picture: _____ square inches

5. Debbie started a table showing a multiplication pattern.

Part A

Complete the table. Describe a pattern you see in the products.

×	1	2	3	4	5	6	7	8	9	10
6	6	12	18							

_____

Part B

If you multiplied 6×73, would the product be an even number or an odd number? Use the table to explain your reasoning.

_____

_____

GO ON

6. Choose the number from the box that makes the sentence true.

Study hall has 63 desks. There are 9 desks in each row.

There are | 7 8 9 | rows of desks in study hall.

7. There were 87 sunflowers at the flower shop in the morning. There were 56 sunflowers left at the end of the day. How many sunflowers were sold? Explain a way to solve the problem.

_____

_____

8. Students at Barnes School are performing in a play. The picture graph shows the number of tickets each class sold so far.

Choose the name from each box that makes the sentence true.

Number of Tickets Sold	
Ms. Brown's Class	✓✓✓✓✓✓✓✓
Mrs. Gold's Class	✓✓✓✓✓
Mr. Castro's Class	✓✓✓✓✓✓

Key: Each ✓ = 5 tickets.

Five fewer tickets were sold by | Ms. Brown's Mrs. Gold's Mr. Castro's |

class than | Ms. Brown's Mrs. Gold's Mr. Castro's | class.

9. Circle numbers to complete the equations.

$$
\begin{array}{|c|}
6 \\
7 \\
8 \\
9 \\
\end{array}
\times 6 = 42
\qquad
42 \div
\begin{array}{|c|}
5 \\
6 \\
7 \\
8 \\
\end{array}
= 6
$$

10. Break apart the array to show $7 \times 5 = (5 \times 2) + (5 \times 5)$.

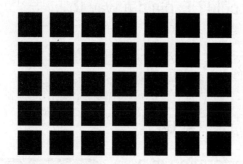

11. The hexagon has been divided into triangles with equal areas. What part of the area of the hexagon is the area of each triangle?

(A) $\frac{1}{4}$

(B) $\frac{2}{6}$

(C) $\frac{1}{3}$

(D) $\frac{1}{6}$

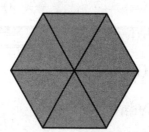

12. Mrs. Park takes the 9:38 A.M. train to the city. The trip takes 3 hours and 20 minutes. What time does Mrs. Park arrive in the city?

_____

GO ON

13. Cody drew this rectangle. Each square unit is 1 square centimeter.

Which equations can Cody use to find the area of the rectangle? Mark all that apply.

Ⓐ $2 + 2 + 2 + 2 + 2 + 2 + 2 + 2 = 16$

Ⓑ $2 + 2 + 2 + 2 + 2 + 2 = 12$

Ⓒ $8 + 8 = 16$

Ⓓ $2 \times 6 = 12$

Ⓔ $8 \times 2 = 16$

Ⓕ $8 + 8 + 8 + 8 + 8 + 8 + 8 + 8 = 64$

14. Julissa makes 4 bracelets. She uses 9 charms on each bracelet.

For numbers 14a–14d, tell if the number sentence could be used to find the number of charms Julissa uses.

14a. $4 + 9 = \blacksquare$ ○ Yes ○ No

14b. $3 + 3 + 3 + 3 = \blacksquare$ ○ Yes ○ No

14c. $9 + 9 + 9 + 9 = \blacksquare$ ○ Yes ○ No

14d. $4 \times 9 = \blacksquare$ ○ Yes ○ No

15. What fraction names point A on the number line?

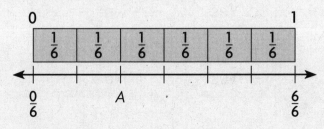

16. Mr. Watson put down new tiles on the floor of his kitchen shown below. What is the area of Mr. Watson's kitchen?

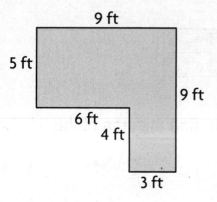

_____ square feet

17. Neil made this multiplication model. Complete the equation that represents the model.

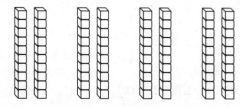

_____ × _____ = _____

18. There are 36 crackers packed in 9 packages with the same number of crackers in each package. How many crackers are in each package?

For numbers 18a–18d, choose Yes or No to tell whether the equation represents the problem.

18a. $9 \times \blacksquare = 36$ ⚪ Yes ⚪ No

18b. $36 + 9 = \blacksquare$ ⚪ Yes ⚪ No

18c. $36 - \blacksquare = 9$ ⚪ Yes ⚪ No

18d. $36 \div \blacksquare = 9$ ⚪ Yes ⚪ No

GO ON

19. Complete the chart to show the quotients.

÷	63	72	90	81
9				

20. Fifteen people are going rafting. They brought 5 rafts.
An equal number of people ride in each raft. How many
people will be in each raft?

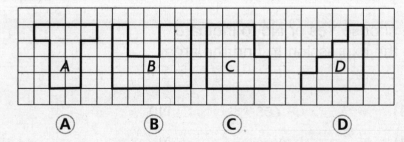

_____ people

21. Find the perimeter of each figure on the grid. Identify
the figures that have a perimeter of 16 units. Mark all
that apply.

Ⓐ   Ⓑ   Ⓒ   Ⓓ

GO ON ➡

22. What is the area of the figure shown? Each unit square is 1 square inch.

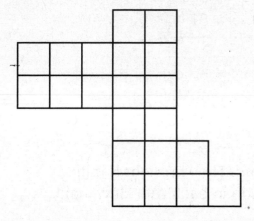

_____ square inches

23. Jen wants to find the area of the large rectangle by adding the areas of the two small rectangles.

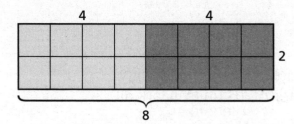

For numbers 23a–23d, choose Yes or No to indicate whether Jen could use the expression to find the area of the large rectangle.

23a. $(8 \times 2) + (8 \times 4)$ ○ Yes   ○ No

23b. $(2 \times 4) + (2 \times 4)$ ○ Yes   ○ No

23c. $(4 \times 2) + (4 \times 2)$ ○ Yes   ○ No

23d. $8 + 8$ ○ Yes   ○ No

GO ON ➡

At the Beach

Solve the problems below using what you know about time, measurement, and geometric shapes.

1. Dasha's family goes to the beach. The clocks show the times the family drives in the morning, has lunch, and leaves the beach.

   a. Write the times using A.M. and P.M.

Morning 	Lunch 	Afternoon 
_____	_____	_____

   b. After leaving the beach, the family gets to the boardwalk at 3:58. How long did it take them to get there? Use a number line to solve.

   ← ─────────────────────────────── →

   _____ minutes

GO ON ➡

2. While at the beach, Dasha uses this bucket to make
sand castles. She fills the bucket 8 times with water.

   a. How many liters of water does she use? Write an
   equation to solve.

                                                      _____ liters

   b. Dasha fills 2 smaller pails with all of the water in one
   bucket. How much water might each small pail hold?
   Draw a picture. Label how much each pail holds.

   c. Suppose Dasha has 217 grams of sand in the bucket
   and 146 grams of shells. What is the mass of the sand
   and the shells? Write an equation to solve.

                                                      _____ grams

3. The boardwalk at the beach has a new bandstand.
The diagram shows the shape of the bandstand.
Each unit square is one square meter. Use the diagram
to solve the problems.

   a. What is the perimeter of the bandstand? Write a
   number sentence to solve.

   b. Break apart the rectangles. Use the Distributive
   Property to find the area of the bandstand. Show your
   work.

4. Workers on the boardwalk are building a new fence
   around the kiddie ride shown in the diagram. They need
   45 feet of fencing. What is the length of the unknown
   side? Show your work.

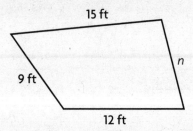

$n =$ _____ feet

5. A new arcade on the boardwalk will have an area of
   18 square meters in the shape of a rectangle.

   a. Draw two ways that the arcade could be shaped.

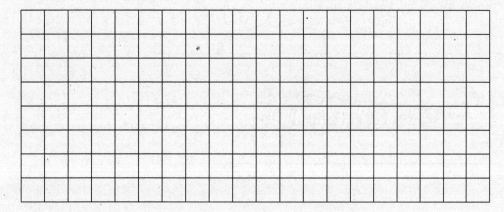

   b. Are the perimeters of the arcades the same?
   Explain your answer.

   _____

   _____

   _____

   _____

GO ON

6. Dasha finds these shells on the beach. Measure each
shell to the nearest $\frac{1}{8}$ inch. Then complete the line plot.

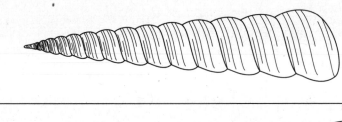

_____

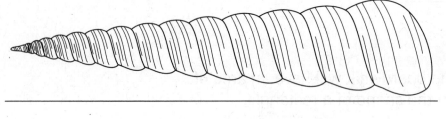

_____

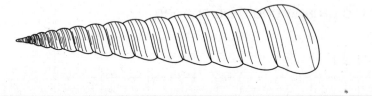

_____

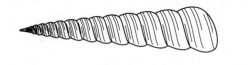

_____

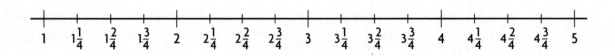

1. Hector is buying books at a bookstore.

Part A

He buys 2 used books and 1 new book for $26. The new book costs $18. Each used book costs the same amount. What is the price of each used book? Explain the steps you use to solve the problem.

_____

_____

Part B

Hector also buys a reading light for $12 and 2 journals for $8 each to give as gifts. Write one equation to describe the total amount Hector spends on gifts. Explain how to use the order of operations to solve the equation.

_____

_____

2. There are 165 cars in the parking lot. Complete the chart to show 165 rounded to the nearest 10.

Hundreds	Tens	Ones

3. Parker divides a fruit bar into 3 equal parts. Circle the word that makes the sentence true.

The fruit bar is divided into

thirds
halves
fourths

GO ON

4. Martin has a poster on his wall that is 4 feet long and 3 feet wide. What is the area of the poster?

Draw a rectangle to help solve the problem. Label your drawing. Write an equation to solve the problem.

Area of the poster: _____ square feet

5. This shows a part of a multiplication table. Find the missing numbers. Explain how you found the numbers.

_____

_____

_____

_____

_____

GO ON

6. For numbers 6a–6d, choose Yes or No to show whether the unknown factor is 8.

6a. $8 \times \blacksquare = 64$ ○ Yes   ○ No

6b. $\blacksquare \times 3 = 27$ ○ Yes   ○ No

6c. $6 \times \blacksquare = 42$ ○ Yes   ○ No

6d. $\blacksquare \times 7 = 56$ ○ Yes   ○ No

7. On Monday, 46 boys and 38 girls bought lunch at school. How many students bought lunch? Explain one way to solve the problem.

_____

_____

8. The bar graph shows the results of a survey of favorite fruits.

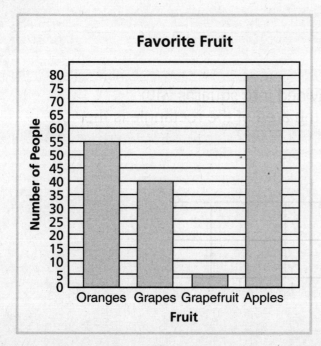

How many more people chose apples than grapes and grapefruit combined?

_____ more people

GO ON

9. Angela plants 24 rosebushes in flowerbeds in her yard. She plants the same number of rosebushes in each of 6 flowerbeds.

Draw circles in these groups to model the problem.

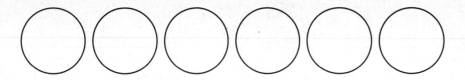

How many rosebushes does Angela plant in each flowerbed?

_____ rosebushes

10. Deanna, Amy, and Pam pick the same number of peaches at an orchard. They each set their peaches in 4 equal piles with 6 peaches in each pile.

Write a multiplication sentence that shows how many peaches they picked.

_____

11. The rectangle has been divided into squares with equal areas. What part of the area of the rectangle is the area of each square?

Ⓐ $\frac{1}{8}$

Ⓑ $\frac{1}{4}$

Ⓒ $\frac{1}{6}$

Ⓓ $\frac{8}{8}$

12. Luz left for the park at 2:27 P.M. She arrived at 3:09 P.M. How long did it take Luz to get to the park?

_____ minutes

GO ON

13. Rory is placing square tiles on the floor of his bathroom. Each unit square is 1 square foot.

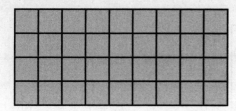

Which equations can Rory use to find the area of the bathroom floor? Mark all that apply.

Ⓐ $4 + 4 + 4 + 4 + 4 = 20$ Ⓓ $4 \times 9 = 36$

Ⓑ $9 \times 4 = 36$ Ⓔ $9 + 9 + 9 + 9 + 9 = 45$

Ⓒ $9 + 9 + 9 + 9 = 36$ Ⓕ $5 \times 9 = 45$

14. Select the number sentences that represent the model. Mark all that apply.

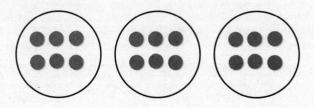

Ⓐ $3 + 6 = 9$ Ⓒ $3 \times 6 = 18$

Ⓑ $6 + 6 + 6 = 18$ Ⓓ $6 + 3 = 9$

15. What fraction names point *A* on the number line?

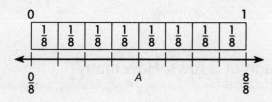

GO ON ➡

16. Kylie and her father planted a new garden shown below. What is the area of the garden?

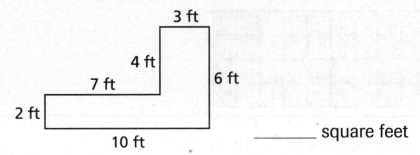

_____ square feet

17. Nick made this multiplication model. Complete the equation that represents the model.

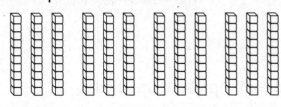

_____ × _____ = _____

18. Circle numbers to complete the related facts.

4
7
8
35

× 5 = 40   40 ÷

4
8
9
45

= 5

19. Dean plants 7 corn plants in each of 5 rows. How many corn plants does Dean plant?

_____ plants

GO ON

20. Enrique started a table showing a division pattern.

÷	10	20	30	40
10				
5				

Part A

Complete the table.

Compare the quotients when dividing by 10 and when dividing by 5. Describe a pattern you see in the quotients.

_____

Part B

Find the quotient, *a*.

$80 \div 10 = a$

$a =$ _____

Find the value of *n*.

$80 \div 5 = n$

$n =$ _____

How could you use *a* to find the value of *n*?

_____

21. Glenda used square tiles to make a rectangle. The rectangle has a perimeter of 8 units and an area of 4 square units. Which could be Glenda's rectangle?

Ⓐ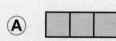

Ⓒ

Ⓑ

Ⓓ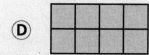

GO ON ➡

22. What is the area of the figure shown? Each unit
square is 1 square meter.

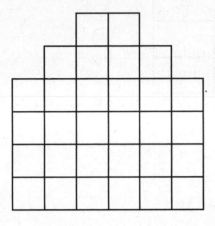

_____ square meters

23. Felicia wants to find the area of the large rectangle by
adding the areas of the two small rectangles.

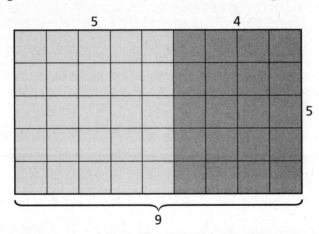

For numbers 23a–23d, choose Yes or No to show
whether Felicia could use the expression to find the area
of the large rectangle.

23a. $(5 \times 4) + (5 \times 5)$ ○ Yes   ○ No

23b. $(9 \times 5) + (9 \times 4)$ ○ Yes   ○ No

23c. $25 + 20$ ○ Yes   ○ No

23d. $(5 \times 5) + (4 \times 5)$ ○ Yes   ○ No

GO ON ▶

Making Quilts

**The third grade art class is making quilts. Solve the problems
below using what you know about geometric shapes.**

1. Carly wants to make a block print for the quilt. She wants to draw a closed
   shape with 5 line segments and two right angles. Draw the shape. Label the
   right angles. Name the shape.

   a. How many angles in the shape are greater than a right angle? _____

   b. How many angles in the shape are less than a right angle? _____

   c. How many sets of perpendicular lines did you draw? _____

   d. How many sets of parallel lines did you draw? _____

   e. Did you draw any intersecting lines? Explain.

   _____

   _____

   _____

2. Carly wants to change the shape to make a hexagon. Explain how she
   can do this.

   _____

   _____

   _____

   _____

   _____

3. Darnell uses block prints to make this design for the quilt.
Study the diagram to answer the questions.

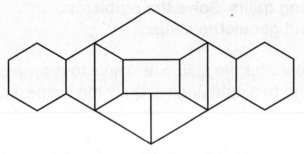

a. How many shapes have right angles? _____

b. How many shapes have perpendicular lines? _____

c. Put an H on the hexagons. Are the hexagons also quadrilaterals?
Explain.

_____

_____

_____

d. Classify the shapes. Complete the chart to show how
many there are of each shape.

Triangles	Quadrilaterals	Rhombuses	Pentagons

4. Ricky makes a design for the quilt. The shape
is a quadrilateral that is not a square. It has
4 sides that are of equal length. Draw the
quadrilateral on the grid. Name the shape.

_____

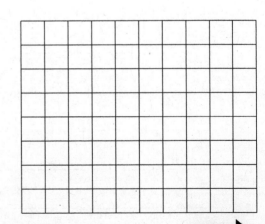

GO ON ➡

5. Draw four shapes to put on the quilt. Classify them using a
Venn diagram. Draw two shapes in each part of the diagram.

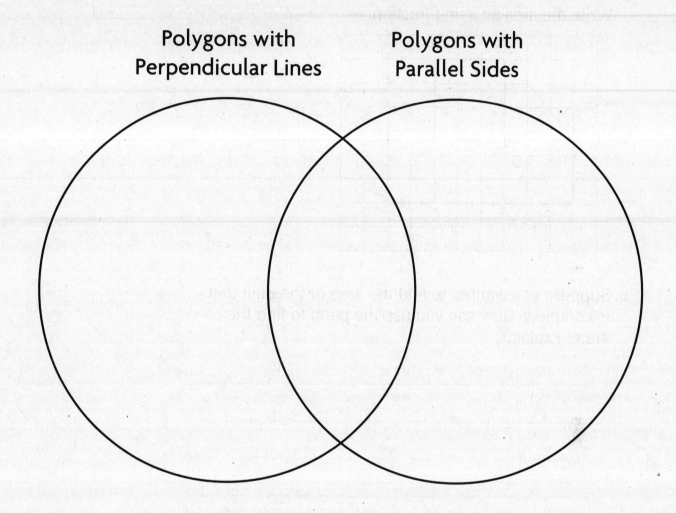

Polygons with
Perpendicular Lines

Polygons with
Parallel Sides

Write the name of the shapes in the section where the
circles overlap.

GO ON

6. The diagram below shows the parts of the quilt that are completed.

    a. Draw to divide the shapes into parts with equal areas. Write the area as a unit fraction.

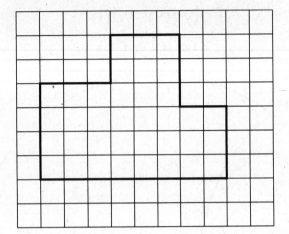

_____

    b. Suppose you wanted to find the area of the quilt that is complete. How can you use the parts to find the area? Explain.

_____

_____

_____

_____

7. Sara makes this block print. How can she divide the shape into 3 rhombuses? Draw to show. Write the area as a unit fraction.

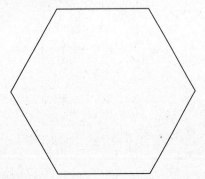

_____

STOP

Planting a Garden

Mrs. Phillips's third grade class is planting a vegetable garden for their school. Mrs. Phillips drew a map of the garden. Each unit square is 1 square meter.

Vegetable Garden:

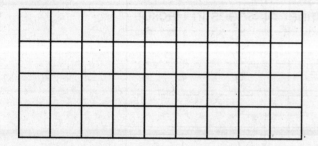

Mrs. Phillips chose the vegetables to plant in the garden. The students then took a survey to find which vegetable their classmates like the most. The table below shows the results of the survey.

Favorite Vegetable	
Carrot	Ж||| I
Lettuce	III
Squash	Ж||| I
Tomato	Ж||| III
Cucumber	IIII
Eggplant	II

GO ON ➡

Mrs. Phillips went to the gardening store to buy seeds to plant each vegetable. She can buy packets of seeds for each vegetable. The table below shows the number of seeds in each packet. One seed is used to plant one of each vegetable.

Packets of Seeds	
Vegetables	Number of Seeds in Packet
Carrot	8
Lettuce	9
Squash	4
Tomato plant	7
Cucumber	6
Eggplant	2

1. How can Mrs. Phillips's students use the Distributive Property to find the area of the garden? Write a number sentence to help you solve. Use drawings to show your answer.

_____

_____

_____

2. Mrs. Phillips's class wants to build a fence around the garden. How many meters will the fence be? Write a number sentence to solve. Show your work.

_____

_____

GO ON ►

3. Mrs. Phillips wants to plant another garden with
the same area but a different perimeter. Use the
grid to draw another garden with the same area as
Mrs. Phillips's garden.

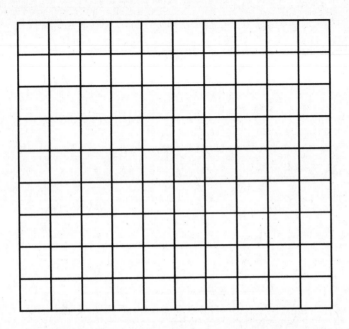

Compare the perimeter of the garden you drew and the perimeter
of the garden Mrs. Phillips drew. How are they different?

_____

_____

_____

_____

_____

4. How do you know that the garden in Mrs. Phillips's
drawing is a rectangle and not a rhombus?

_____

_____

_____

_____

5. Mrs. Phillips's class wants to divide the garden into rectangles with equal areas. Each rectangle will be used for one vegetable.

   a. How many vegetables are the students planting?

   _____

   b. Draw lines to divide the garden into equal parts for each vegetable.

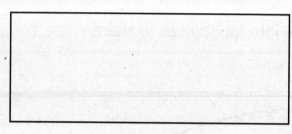

Vegetable Garden

   c. What part of the area of the garden is the area of each rectangle? Write your answer as a fraction.

   _____

6. In one part of the garden, the students want to plant 28 cucumbers. What is the least number of packets of seeds the students need to buy to plant the cucumbers? Are there any seeds left over? Use drawings to show your answer.

_____

_____

7. In another part of the garden, the students want to plant 42 tomato plants. How many packets of tomato plant seeds do the students need to plant the tomato plants? Write an equation to solve. Show your work.

_____

_____

_____

8. Julie wants to divide a carrot into four pieces to share with her friends.

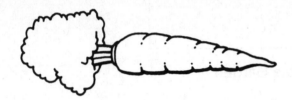

a. What fraction of the carrot does each person get?

_____

b. Julie takes two pieces of the carrot. What fraction of the carrot does Julie have? Show the fraction as the sum of unit fractions.

_____

c. Kaylee has $\frac{2}{6}$ of a carrot. Jorge has $\frac{2}{3}$ of a carrot. Which student has a larger piece of carrot? Shade the fraction bars below to solve. Write a comparison sentence.

0   1
| $\frac{1}{6}$ | $\frac{1}{6}$ | $\frac{1}{6}$ | $\frac{1}{6}$ | $\frac{1}{6}$ | $\frac{1}{6}$ |

0   1
| $\frac{1}{3}$ | $\frac{1}{3}$ | $\frac{1}{3}$ |

_____